www.WellTraveledSquirrel.com

The Story
(in a nutshell)

Tommy the squirrel wakes up to find that his home has been transported to New York City and is now the famous Rockefeller Center Christmas Tree. A stranger in a strange land, Tommy must figure out a way to conquer his fears and explore his new world.

And thus begins the adventures of...

The Most Well-Traveled Squirrel in the Whole Wide World!

— To our loving and supportive families and friends. —
We hope Tommy inspires you the way
you inspire us!

The forest was quiet, not much to be heard
from any tree, owl, pond, or bird.

The fog sat quietly and the night set in.
The forest sighed heavily and deep from within.

The branches swayed slightly in the calm evening breeze
as a young baby deer let out a big sneeze: *"Achoo!"*

The pond's water rippled out from the edge
as a branch fell in from a nearby hedge.

All was peaceful and all was silent.
No one expected to hear something so violent!

Off in the distance a thundering growl sounded
that made all the animals a bit confounded!

The creature moved forward—slowly at first—
its eyes pierced the darkness, but that's not the worst!

Closer and closer, it made the ground shake
and rattled almost every animal awake!

They all rushed off as they heard the creature grind;
so quickly, in fact, that someone was left behind!

He snored through all the noise and hullabaloo,
getting some sleep that was long overdue.

"10! 9! 8!" they began to cry.

And onward they shouted,
"7! 6! 5!"

The crowd continued with a "4!" and a "3!"
with so many smiles and much jubilee.

The countdown was ending—but not the fun—
as they all screamed together "2! 1!"

Tommy shuddered as
a rainbow hit his eyes.
The colors were blinding—
a bit of a surprise.

His room had no windows
for light to get through.
How could this be?
He hadn't a clue.

Tommy took a step and his instincts kicked in.
He grabbed a branch as his head began to spin.

This was no dream; he was not alone...
Where was his forest?

Where was his home?

Many smells filled his nose,
and colors danced in his eyes:

Different kinds of clothing,

hot cocoa,

and french fries.

With all these new things, Tommy could not think—
then suddenly he saw an ice skating rink!

Rounded at the edges...a sweet, shiny white.
Tommy realized that he could not stay up at this height.

He wanted—no, *needed*—to investigate this place
that put a bright smile on everyone's face.

So Tommy ran down
the Norway Spruce tree,

and hid out of sight
under all the debris.

He ran toward the rink
with much unrest;
and when he looked up,
his heart **leapt** from
his chest.

12

In all of its splendor and all of its might,
Tommy struggled to keep it all in his sight.

Right before him was a *beautiful,*
colorful,
tremendous marquee—

The Rockefeller Center Christmas Tree!

All of this scenery took Tommy by surprise.
To the left! To the right! He darted his eyes.

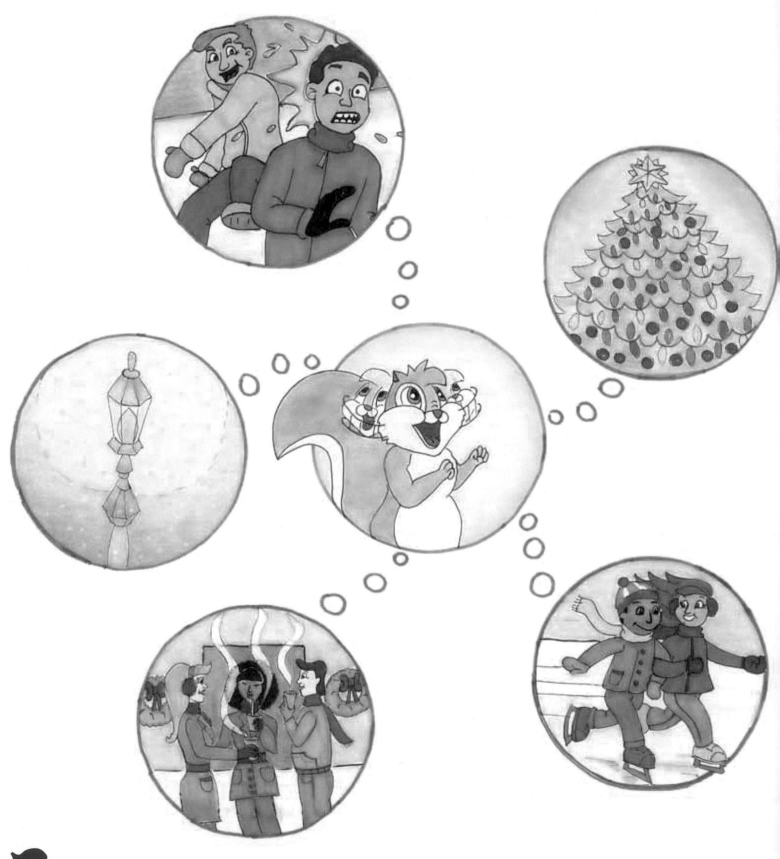

The **children:** playing like him and his brother.

The **tree:** lights shining on one another.

The **people:** floating around on the ice.

And **others:** drinking what smelled like pumpkin spice.

The **snow:** trickling down, lit up by a street light;

Everything filled Tommy with such delight!

But Tommy came to realize, as he let out a groan—

He was a long, long, **long** way from home.

Tommy lunged forward
and ran in full stride.
He jumped on the ice
and started to slide!

With all four feet
sprawled this way and that,
Tommy struggled mightily to...
avoid a charging cat!

The feline, named Jerome,
ran right into the squirrel.
And both furry creatures
started to twirl.

In that instant,
Tommy did not have
to think twice.
He arose very quickly
and ran off the ice!

The squirrel sprinted away, running for many blocks.
He could not tell if that was a cat or a fox!

18

Eventually Tommy found
his way back to his tree
and for the next few weeks
only explored as far as he could see.
He would come down to nibble when
something dropped on the ground.
(His taste in food was not
very profound!)

Then, one brisk evening,
Tommy left the tree for
good.

And began on a journey
like that of Robin Hood!

After walking for a bit,
Tommy noticed from his perch,
a big red glow coming from
the top of a church.

He ran toward the building as fast as he could
and scaled up to the roof where a large sleigh stood.

Nine heads nodded downward to a small open space,
with one of the nine showing bright red on his face.

Tommy took their signal and raced through the hole,
he could sense he was near some kind of a goal.

Tumbling down in darkness,
Tommy landed with a **"Poof!"**
And looked straight up at a
man in a big red suit.

"Ho! Ho! Ho!" the man cried.
"What have we here?"
"This isn't one of my trusty
reindeer!"

"I'm Tommy, sir," he shyly replied,
"A simple squirrel scared out of his hide."
                "Do not worry," the man said.
                "And do not fear.
                This is a church, after all—
                        and you're always
                        welcome here!"

The church, St. Patrick's Cathedral, was very large indeed.
There was nothing like it in the world, both of them agreed!

As they walked, the two shared their life stories:
- The **woes**, the **worries**;
- The **triumphs**, the **glories**.

Tommy was a small squirrel, far away from home
who felt even smaller under the cathedral's large dome.

Santa was a man as old as time
the subject of many nursery rhymes.
Tall and round, he was always very jolly
and smelled like chimneys,
candy canes, and holly.

"Pardon me, sir,"
Tommy said shyly (his tail in a curl).
"I thought you only visited the homes of young
boys and girls?"

"Well," Santa replied, "Christmas is about so much more than getting good grades or doing your chores.

It's about helping those less fortunate than you or me. Children with less things—or even no family."

"And, well—you may have heard
some call me 'Jolly Old St. Nick.'
I like to stop here on my feast day
to hang with my dear friend, St. Patrick!"

Santa then sat down in a chair lined with silk
and the two of them shared more
stories over cookies and milk.

Once they were down to
the very last crumb,
the man asked Tommy
where he was from.

Santa could see the
turmoil in Tommy's eyes
as the homesick squirrel
struggled to reply.

"Hmm," said Santa. "I know how you feel.
The mix of emotions can be very surreal."

"You're excited and awake yet worried and tired.
These past few weeks were much more than you desired."

Santa then said, "Whenever you feel afraid,
ring this acorn bell, and happiness will come to your aid."

"It is no ordinary bell and makes no ordinary sound—
for when you use it, good thoughts will abound!"

With that, Tommy let Santa lead the way
as they returned to the roof and Santa's big sleigh.

Tommy thought hard about what Santa had taught him:
That sometimes it is okay to be out on a limb.

For if he always stayed so close to his childhood tree,
he would never become all the squirrel he could be.

Filled with a new outlook and
a bit of common sense
Tommy heard some bells
off in the distance.

Within seconds dear Santa was flying right by,
guiding his reindeer through the dark night sky.
They swooped near Tommy, along with some birds
and Santa left Tommy with some final, parting words...

"**Merry Christmas** to you, Tommy the Squirrel!"

"The Most **Well-Traveled Squirrel**

in the **Whole Wide World!**"

The End

Glossary:

Abound — [uh-**bound**]: to occur or exist in great quantities or numbers

Confounded — [kon-**foun**-did]: bewildered; confused; perplexed

Debris — [duh-**bree**]: the remains of anything broken down or destroyed; ruins; rubble

Desired — [dih-**zahyuh** rd]: wanted or wished for; coveted

Disarray — [dis-uh-**rey**]: disorder; confusion

Hullabaloo — [**huhl**-uh-buh-**loo**]: a loud noise or disturbance; uproar

Instincts — [**in**-stin(k)z]: natural abilities to know what to do in a particular situation

Investigate — [in-**ves**-ti-geyt]: to observe or study closely

Jubilee — [**joo**-buh-**lee**]: an occasion of rejoicing or festivity

Marquee — [mahr-**kee**]: A large projection (usually a signboard) over the entrance of a theater or other building that highlights an event or the building itself

Outlook — [out-**look**]: mental attitude or view; point of view

Proceeded — [pruh-**seed-did**]: moved or went forward, especially after stopping

Profound — [pruh-**found**]: having deep insight; difficult to understand

Splendor — [**splen**-der]: brilliant or gorgeous appearance, coloring, etc.; magnificence

Surreal — [suh-**reel**]: unbelievable; fantastic; dreamlike

Turmoil — [tur-**moil**] : a state or condition of extreme confusion

* Definition sources - dictionary.com and merriam-webster.com